Proper, Poised & Polished: The Power of You

Proper, Poised & Polished:
The Power of You

AN A TO Z GUIDE TO BECOMING YOUR UNIQUE, PERSONAL BEST

Patricia Napier-Fitzpatrick

The Etiquette School of New York in Manhattan and Southampton
243 Elm Street, Southampton, NY 11968

Editor: Nanci Alderman

Visit my Web site at www.etiquette-ny.com

ISBN-13: 9780692753453
ISBN-10: 0692753451

FIRST EDITION: May 2017

For My Daughter, Kelly
My Sisters, Mary and Peggy
My Nieces, Ashley, Megan, Lindsey,
Madeleine, Meg, Morgan, and Delilah

And for every girl and woman who aspires
to be her own unique, personal best

Table of Contents

Introduction

I have always been interested in proper behavior, appearance, poise, drive, and being the best one can be. Life is what we make it. It doesn't just happen; it takes work. Of course to me, it doesn't often seem like work because I have always enjoyed the process of doing everything I can to be my own unique, personal best. What about you?

Whatever you decide to do or become, the path will be much more assured if you are proper, poised, and polished. The power these three traits will bring you is undeniable. Knowing how to properly conduct yourself in the business and social arenas; being able to make polite conversation; dressing in a stylish and appropriate way wherever you go; carrying yourself with poise and confidence; and possessing polished socials graces, good manners, formal dining skills, and effective communication skills will give you the power to achieve your goals.

Every girl at one time or another in her childhood has wanted to grow up to be a princess. I was no different. I spent hours walking with a book on my head after watching the move *Gigi*. Of course Gigi wasn't being groomed to be a princess, but her training process was very similar to that of a princess's. I watched *My Fair Lady* and *The Sound of Music* countless times; and with my daughter I watched *Walt Disney's Beauty and the Beast, Cinderella* and *The Princess Diaries* with the same sense of awe I had as a young girl.

An ordinary girl can grow up to be a princess—a tale as old as time. Today there are a number of women in the world who did not come from royal backgrounds, but are now princesses. So it seems possible for all of us. Why not me you might ask yourself. Of course, being groomed for the corner office is the dream of most young women now. My finishing school prepares women for both roles.

The joy is in the journey. Think of your life as a glorious adventure, and yourself as a cocoon gradually opening each year of your life until you become this magnificent butterfly.

We are never too old to transform or redefine ourselves. I am older now, but I am still striving to be my unique personal best. Just like etiquette, I am always evolving.

Many older adults have asked me if they are too old to attend a finishing school. My answer is always you are never too old to learn something new or to reinvent yourself. How boring we would be if we stayed the same throughout our lives—n'est-ce pas?

Proper, Poised and Polished: The Power of You is an A to Z guide to transforming yourself to become your unique, personal best. With this book, I hope to inspire you with my carefully curated selection of quotes from accomplished, inspiring, and iconic people, along with empowering tips to guide you along your path to your own transformation from the person you are today to the person you aspire to be tomorrow.

Appearance

Appearance: The way that someone or something looks;
an impression given by someone.

*Appearance counts for 55% of a first impression.
Your looks may be the first impression a stranger
has about you, and so they play a bigger role at a
first meeting than they do at later meetings.*
Nicholas Boothman

*When others look at the way you dress,
they make conclusions about you.
Every time you dress well, you positively influence
the way you are perceived.*
Joe Vitale

*Like gift wrapping, the more "put together"
your appearance, the more you leave
a positive impression.*
Michael Levine

*Look the part by dressing
to the level of power you aspire.
If you speak eloquently, dress well,
and back it up with the social skills
to put others at ease,
virtually no group will exclude you.*
Camille Lavington

*Wearing the correct dress for any occasion
is a matter of good manners.*
Loretta Young

A lady knows that her posture is as important
as any article of clothing on her back.
Candace Simpson-Giles

Regular exercise gives you a healthy,
glowing look and an unmistakable
va-va-voom that you just
can't get any other way.
Catherine Guthrie

PNF: Before you say a word, your appearance has already announced who you are to the world. Your first impression is made in only seconds and yet it may follow you indefinitely. Your appearance is more than the way you dress: It includes your grooming and your body language—your posture, the way you walk, your facial expression and the tone of your voice—all of which reinforce the positive impression of your attire or leave a conflicting or negative impression. As Pamela Fiori, past editor-in-chief of "Town & Country," advises: "Throw your shoulders back, straighten your posture, and look ahead, not down. And, look the part and you will deserve to play it."

Empowering Tips

1 DRESS APPROPRIATELY. Wearing attire appropriate for an occasion not only shows respect for the host and other guests, but also for the event itself. Some say being over-dressed is better than being underdressed, but I say being appropriately dressed will make you and the others attending an event feel comfortable—and that is good manners.

2 LOOK THE PART. It is very simple: you have to look the part to get the part—what-ever part it is that you want to get. It's about being credible; it's about having presence. Of course, it is understood that you will have the knowledge or skills to do the part (job). Package yourself for success!

3 POLISH YOUR APPEARANCE. Being polished and groomed is rated as the most important aspect of appearance, according to research. Polish your shoes. Polish your nails. Polish your teeth. These are good grooming musts. A polished appearance will open doors wherever you go, and it will get you invited back!

4 GET FIT. Being fit, strong, and healthy will not only make you look and feel better, it will enable you to exude a healthy glow, which is always attractive; and looking fit signals that you have the energy and strength to successfully handle whatever comes your way.

5 STAND UP STRAIGHT; NEVER SLOUCH. Good posture will add more to the perception of your appearance than any other factor. It gives the impression of confidence and poise. All items of clothing are enhanced through good carriage; and it can make you look ten years younger and ten pounds lighter. When you are walking, keep your head level—not too high, not too low.

Beauty

Beauty: The quality present in a thing or
person that gives intense pleasure
or deep satisfaction to the mind.

*For beautiful eyes, look for the good in others;
for beautiful lips, speak only words of kindness;
and for poise, walk with the knowledge
that you are never alone.*
Audrey Hepburn

*Then they [good manners] must be inspired
by the good heart.
There is no beautifier or complexion,
or form, or behavior, like the wish
to scatter good joy and not pain around us.*
Ralph Waldo Emerson

*Beauty is when you can appreciate yourself.
When you love yourself, that's when
you're most beautiful.*
Zoe Kravitz

*I think that women who know who
they are are beautiful.*
Demi Lovato

*Love yourself. It is important to stay positive
because beauty comes from the inside out.*
Jenn Proske

Beauty is not in the face;
beauty is a light in the heart.
Kahlil Gibran

A thing of beauty is a joy forever:
its loveliness increases;
it will never pass into nothingness.
John Keats

PNF: When I was a child, I was often told that beauty is as beauty does. Physical beauty is a bonus if you have it, but confidence and a delightful personality trump beauty! If you show that you are comfortable with your appearance, others will be also. Make the most of your assets and walk with a confident air that says, "I value myself." Jackie Kennedy Onassis wasn't classically beautiful, and yet everyone thought she was. Nor is Sarah Jessica Parker, but she exudes confidence, making us think she is beautiful.

Empowering Tips

1 BE A BEAUTIFUL PERSON INSIDE. A beautiful person knows that beauty alone is not enough to "win friends and influence people." Showing interest in others is what will ultimately win people over and make them want to date you, be their friend, or do business with you.

2 MIND YOUR MANNERS. Beautiful manners will always make a good impression and will never go out of style. Beautiful manners include being kind, considerate and respectful—always making others around you feel comfortable–and never intentionally embarrassing anyone.

3 HIGHLIGHT YOUR UNIQUE ASSETS. We are each beautiful in our own way. Accept what you cannot change about yourself; make the most of what is beautiful about you and focus on attracting attention to it, whether it be your hair, your eyes, your smile, your vitality, or even your unusual looks.

4 ACCEPT COMPLIMENTS GRACIOUSLY. A simple "Thank you" will do. If you try to negate a compliment, it implies the person paying the compliment has questionable taste. Don't think you have to parrot back the compliment either. If, however, you were planning to tell the person how much you like her dress, or how well she looks, and she complimented you first, by all means reciprocate.

5 POISE WILL MAKE YOU MORE BEAUTIFUL. A woman who walks with grace, elegance and confidence can make heads turn without any other effort. Poise is power.

Confidence

Confidence: A feeling of self-assurance
arising from one's appreciation
of one's own abilities or qualities.

Believe in yourself.
Have faith in your abilities!
Without a humble but reasonable confidence
in your own powers you cannot
be successful or happy.
Norman Vincent Peale

There is a quality [confidence] that
sets some people apart.
It is hard to define but easy to recognize.
With it, you can take on the world; without it,
you live stuck in the starting block of
your personality.
Katty Kay and Claire Shipman

Optimism is the faith that leads to achievement.
Nothing can be done without hope and confidence.
Helen Keller

Confidence is contagious.
So is lack of confidence.
Vince Lombardi

Being glamorous is about strength and confidence.
It's black and white—dramatic. You have to be strong.
Catherine Zeta-Jones

If you're presenting yourself with confidence,
you can pull off pretty much anything.
Katy Perry

I think confidence is the most appealing quality
in any human being or artist;
that's what really attracts us to people.
Marilyn Manson

PNF: Confidence in your abilities or qualities is essential if you want to be successful. Self-assurance will give you the courage to achieve your goals and reach your highest potential. You can build confidence by accepting challenges, trying new things, overcoming obstacles, and staying with something until you succeed.

Malala Yousafzai, the youngest-ever Nobel Prize laureate, had complete and utter confidence in her conviction that girls should be allowed to go to school and receive an education, and it gave her the courage to stand up for her beliefs against all odds in her native country of Pakistan.

Empowering Tips

1 LEARN THE RULES OF ETIQUETTE TO BUILD CONFIDENCE. The rules of etiquette are like a road map through life. When we know we are on the right road, it makes us feel confident that we will successfully arrive at our destination.

2 FOLLOW THE ACT FORMULA TO BUILD CONFIDENCE. Here's how: **A**=Action: Try new things and overcome obstacles. As you do, you will build the confidence you will need to succeed. **C=Courage:** To act before you have confidence requires courage. You can get courage from other people, from books, from other resources, and from creating it within yourself. **T=Target:** To assure your success, you must have a clear target to shoot at—a clear picture of what you want to accomplish or acquire.

3 CONFIDENCE WILL ATTRACT OTHERS TO YOU. Having confidence in yourself is a very attractive quality to possess, until it crosses over to arrogance. People are drawn to, and want to follow, confident people. They are not drawn to those who are arrogant or conceited. When you have a healthy level of confidence, employers are more likely to trust you with a project, knowing that you will be good at motivating others.

4 DEFINE YOUR PERSONAL BRAND. When a person exudes confidence, we want to work with them, and we are more likely to follow their lead. William Arruda, a personal branding expert, says confidence is important because it is the most attractive personal brand attribute. "Confidence is the number one byproduct of the personal branding process, because in branding you uncover what makes you exceptional and use it to make career choices and deliver outstanding value."

5 KNOW YOUR MATERIAL. Practice makes perfect. Practice builds confidence. The more you practice a speech, a toast, a presentation, the more confident you will be that it will turn out well and be positively received. Confidence comes from truly knowing your material.

Diligence

Diligence: Constant and earnest effort to
accomplish what is undertaken;
persistent exertion of body or mind.

*You really have to work hard and apply yourself,
and by applying yourself and working hard,
and by being diligent, you can achieve success.*
Julie Benz

*Work hard. Laugh when you feel like crying.
Keep an open mind, open eyes, and an open spirit.*
Rachel Ray

*Being the last man standing confirmed my philosophy
that tenacity, hard work, and a lot of good luck
is a combination hard to beat.*
Ira Neimark

*When I believe in something,
I'm like a dog with a bone.*
Melissa McCarthy

*Working hard becomes a habit,
a serious kind of fun.
You get self-satisfaction
from pushing yourself to the limit,
knowing that all the effort is going to pay off.*
Mary Lou Retton

I was obliged to be industrious.
Whoever is equally industrious
will succeed equally well.
Johann Sebastian Bach

I am a perfectionist, and I always think
I can do better what I've done, even if it's good.
Luciano Pavarotti

PNF: Anyone who is successful knows that success takes hard work and determination. It also takes planning and a clear vision for the future. By beginning with the end in mind, formulating a plan, and working patiently and diligently toward achieving it, you *will* be successful.

Diane Sawyer waited two decades for her chance to anchor ABC's "World News Tonight." She graciously stayed the course, and it paid off: She became the anchor in December 2009, and held that position until September 2014. Katy Perry had many unsuccessful attempts at being commercially successful until she succeeded with her hit single, "I Kissed a Girl." And I believe everyone knows the story of J.K. Rowling, the author of *Harry Potter*. It took her five years to finish the book, only to have it rejected by twelve major publishers. Finally, a small publishing company agreed to publish it. Today her books have been translated into 79 languages and have sold more than 450 million copies throughout the world!

Empowering Tips

1 SET GOALS. It is much easier to be diligent when you have a plan or goal to achieve. Set small achievable goals that will lead you to your larger goal. Set a specific timetable, not just a deadline, for achieving these goals. When you do achieve a goal, congratulate yourself. Although nice, we shouldn't always need to have recognition from others before we feel good about our accomplishments.

2 PRACTICE, PRACTICE, PRACTICE. Productive and successful people are extremely diligent; they practice the things that are important to them on a consistent basis. As an example, for top performers, it is not about the performance per se, but about the continual practice. If there is something you would like to get better at, such as playing a musical instrument, it will take many hours of dedicated practice. If you are unhappy about having to devote so much time to a particular endeavor, interest, or job, perhaps you should pursue a different one.

3 WORK HARD TO BUILD GOOD HABITS. Human beings are creatures of habit; we become what we repeatedly do. Building good habits is a process; and according to the latest research on the subject, it takes 66 days to form a habit, not 21 days as previously thought. The nice thing about good habits, however, is that once formed they become automatic. Although conversely, bad habits also become automatic, and can prevent you from becoming the person you would most like to be.

4 RESIST PROCRASTINATION. Procrastination is the number one enemy of perseverance. Each time you can resist procrastinating, you become more diligent. Studies show that those who are able to delay gratification are more successful in life. Ignore the temptation to do something else when you have something that needs to be done: Finish a project, practice the piano, or go to the gym *before* you do something that might be more fun. Focus on the success you will achieve and the joy you will feel if you keep your word to yourself.

5 **BE SELFLESS IN HELPING OTHERS.** Be a team player, and be diligent about helping others. Pitch in when they could use your help—whether it is at your own home, a guest in someone else's home, or at the office. It shows consideration for others; and it will make them want to gladly help you when you need their help with something.

Etiquette

Etiquette: Conventional requirements as to
social behavior; proprieties of conduct
as established in any class or
community or for any occasion.

*Nothing is less important
than which fork you use.
Etiquette is the science of living.
It embraces everything.
It is ethics. It is honor.*
Emily Post

*Good manners will open doors
that the best education cannot.*
Clarence Thomas

*Fine manners need the support
of fine manners in others.*
Ralph Waldo Emerson

*Once I said to my mother,
'You would be happy
if I just kept well dressed and
had good manners,' and she said:
'What else is there?'*
Cy Twombly

*You can get through life with bad manners,
but it's easier with good manners.*
Lillian Gish

In England, we have such good manners that
if someone says something impolite,
the police will get involved.
Russell Brand

I make a distinction between manners and etiquette—
manners as the principles, which are eternal
and universal; etiquette as the particular rules
which are arbitrary and different in different times,
different situations, different cultures.
Judith Martin

PNF: In today's cosmopolitan, global environment, it is important to know the rules of etiquette and protocol. Fine manners are a must! Learn how to make proper introductions; how to correctly conduct yourself in all of the various situations in which you find yourself; how to make polite conversation; how to graciously enter and exit conversations; how to dine with finesse. And be cognizant of business protocol if you are a business professional. Knowing these rules will make you more confident, and make others feel more at ease when they are around you.

Empowering Tips

1 **MAKE SOCIAL INTRODUCTIONS ACCORDING TO AGE AND GENDER**. Social etiquette is based upon respect and courtesy. In the social arena, introductions should be made according to age and gender. A woman's name is spoken before a man's—unless he is much older. If a man is much older, his name is spoken first, and the younger person is presented to him.

2 **MAKE BUSINESS INTRODUCTIONS ACCORDING TO HIERARCHY.** In business, gender is not a factor in introductions. The name of the most important person is spoken first; the name of the person with less authority is spoken last and is presented to the person with more authority.

3 **RESPECT THE PERSON IN FRONT OF YOU.** This means that the person you're with takes precedence over technological devices. Although technology is most often blamed for the decline in manners in our modern-day world, it is using it at an inappropriate time or place that makes us rude.

4 **BE A LOYAL FRIEND.** To have friends, you must first be a friend. A loyal friend means that you are there for them when they need you; you do not gossip or talk about them behind their backs; and it means they can trust you to keep your word.

5 **SHOW RESPECT FOR DIFFERENCES.** Courtesy for others whose beliefs, culture, or color are different from yours is of the utmost importance today. Better still, embrace the differences, and realize it is our differences that make the world interesting.

Fashion

Fashion: A popular trend, especially
in styles of dress and ornament
or manners of behavior.

I don't design clothes, I design dreams.
Ralph Lauren

*Fashion is not something that exists in dresses only.
Fashion is in the sky, in the street; fashion has to do
with ideas, the way we live, what is happening.*
Coco Chanel

*It's important to find out what really
suits who you are, because style isn't
only what you wear, it's what you project.*
Carolina Herrera

*The Parisian never worships fashion idols.
She is a fashion icon in her own right.*
Ines de la Fressange

*We've come a long way. Power dressing
now is designed to let the women inside
us come through.*
Donna Karan

*Since I was young, the artistic expression
that fashion embodies has inspired me.
It's a way to communicate oneself.*
Maria Sharpova

I believe my clothes can give people
a better image of themselves—that it
can increase feelings of confidence and happiness.
Giorgio Armani

PNF: Fashion is the ultimate expression of oneself. You reveal who you truly are by the clothes and accessories you choose to wear. Coco Chanel believed that fashion wasn't just about clothing. She preferred to think in terms of style, "the subtle alliance between a garment, a perfume, a piece of jewelry, and a woman's whole demeanor, the way she carried herself and moved," according to Jerome Gautier in his book *Chanel: The Vocabulary of Style.*

Empowering Tips

1 USE YOUR WARDROBE TO INFLUENCE YOUR AUDIENCE. Choosing the appropriate wardrobe is a communication skill, according to image consultant Sylvie di Gusto. She recommends you "Leverage your personal style to influence your audience." Before you have said a word, your clothes and accessories, along with your grooming and body language, have spoken volumes about you.

2 AVOID FASHION NO-NOS. Wrinkled clothes, missing buttons, stains, showing too much cleavage, or wearing clothes that are too tight can all undermine your credibility. Casual clothes may be appropriate for your office or industry, but in their fit, brand, and style, they should communicate that you take yourself and your job seriously. Casual does not mean sloppy.

3 BE MEMORABLE. In businesses known as "white-collar" professional—such as the financial, accounting, and legal fields, you will need to dress conservatively; but that doesn't mean you have to dress in a boring, nondescript way. "If you look fantastic and fashion forward, you'll feel more confident and people will notice and remember you," writes Kate White in her book *I Shouldn't Be Telling You This*.

4 DON'T BE A FASHION VICTIM. Give a nod to fashion each season, rather than wearing every fashion trend from head to toe. Be an original, mixing and matching new clothes and accessories to suit your unique style. You can be reasonably on-trend, especially if you are looking for a job. An outdated look can signal outdated skills.

5 WEAR CLOTHING THAT FLATTERS/ENHANCES YOUR FIGURE. Choose outfits to highlight your assets and downplay any negatives. You may not have perfect proportions but, with the right clothes and the right fit, you can give the illusion that you do.

Genuine

Genuine: Actually having the reputed or
apparent qualities of character;
real, not false.

*Always be a first-rate version of yourself,
instead of a second-rate version of somebody else.*
Judy Garland

*How many cares one loses when one
decides not to be something but to be someone.*
Coco Chanel

*Treat everyone with politeness,
even those who are rude to you—
not because they are nice,
but because you are.*
Author Unknown

*I don't want to play the game.
I want to redefine it.*
Amy Schumer

*I think some people project things on you,
but I'm trying to handle everything around me
with a certain amount of grace,
dignity and good manners.
You just can't necessarily win all the time.*
Katie Couric

Sexiness is all about your personality,
being genuine and confident,
and being a good person.
Erin Heatherton

Cherish forever what makes you unique,
'cuz you're really a yawn if it goes.
Bette Midler

PNF: In the end, it is really your character that matters the most. Character is formed very early in life, which is why a child's family life is so important. The home is where children learn right from wrong, how to treat others, how to take responsibility for their actions, and how to be a team player by pitching in and helping with the chores. As former first lady Michelle Obama said, "With every word we utter, with every action we take, we know our kids are watching us. We as parents are the most important models."

Empowering Tips

1 USE THE MAGIC WORDS. Always be polite, and use the "magic words." The "magic words" are not just for children; these polite words are for everyone. When you say "Please," "Thank you," "You're welcome," "Excuse me," and "I'm sorry" at the right time, you create positive reactions and are perceived to be a genuinely good person.

2 BE HONEST AND TRUSTWORTHY. These are two of the most important qualities for a person to possess; and what your friends, family, and colleagues expect and desire from you.

3 DO THE RIGHT THING. Having good character means doing the right thing simply because it is the right thing to do. Great leaders are judged by their character. Having good character means having such admirable traits as honesty, responsibility, courage, fairness, and trustworthiness.

4 SHOW A SINCERE INTEREST IN OTHERS. When you meet people, show a genuine desire to get to know them. Appreciate them for who they are. Make them feel good about themselves. Only then can you truly discover their authentic selves.

5 BE SOMEONG YOU CAN BE PROUD OF. Think about what you stand for and what your friends and family would say about your character. Are you proud of this image? If not, do something about it. Your good character is one of the most important assets you have, and is revealed by what you do when no one is watching.

Habit

Habit: An acquired mode of behavior that has become nearly or completely involuntary.

Habit is the intersection of knowledge, skill and desire.
It is a process of personal and interpersonal growth.
Stephen Covey

We are what we repeatedly do.
Excellence then is not an act, but a habit.
Aristotle

We first make our habits; then our habits make us.
English poet

Good, better, best. Never let it rest.
Until your good is better and your better best.
Tim Duncan

We all naturally want to become successful…
we also want to take shortcuts. And it's easy to do,
but you can never take away the effort of hard work
and discipline and sacrifice.
Apolo Ohno

Successful people are simply people
with successful habits.
Brian Tracy

*Your net worth to the world's usually
determined by what remains after your
bad habits are subtracted
from your good ones.*
Benjamin Franklin

PNF: To form the habits necessary to be successful takes discipline. When there is something I don't want to do, but know I must—such as go to the gym or answer my emails—I make myself "just do it." And sometimes I think to myself, "Begin with the end in mind," as Stephen Covey advises in his book *The Seven Habits of Highly Effective People*. I think about how good I am going to feel when I have finished at the gym or replied to all the emails I need to answer.

When Frank Lloyd Wright was asked about his success in life, he said, "I know the price of success: dedication, hard work, and an unremitting devotion to the things you want to see happen." Even Michelangelo was to have said: "If people knew how hard I work to gain my mastery, it would not seem so wonderful at all."

Empowering Tips

1 DON'T KEEP PEOPLE WAITING. Make it a habit to be on time when you have a meeting, business appointment, or plans with a friend or family member. Being late can leave a bad impression. Always have your fare card, cash, or ticket out and ready before lining up to board public transportation so that you don't keep those behind you waiting.

2 EAT IN APPROPRIATE PLACES. Make it a habit to eat in restaurants or other suitable places, such as the park—not on buses, the subway, taxis, or walking down the street.

3 BE MINDFUL OF OTHERS IN PUBLIC. Do you ever get annoyed when you have to listen to someone else's cell phone conversation? Remember that can be true for others when you're the one on the phone. Whether it's a business or personal call, you never know who is listening. So make it a habit to be aware of others when you are talking in public; speak softly; and don't discuss professional or private matters within hearing distance of others.

4 PUT YOUR BEST FOOT FORWARD. Make it a habit to do your best in everything you do—if not for yourself, do it for your team or for those who look up to you as a role model.

5 MAINTAIN GOOD HYGIENE. Make it a habit to freshen up before going to an event. In fact, you should always practice good hygiene whenever you are going to be in the presence of other people. Keep deodorant at your office and breath mints with you at all times. Never, however, freshen your breath by chewing gum in public.

Interesting

Interesting: Engaging or exciting and holding
the attention or curiosity.

Learn the principles of storytelling.
Stories are powerful.
Stories are better than statistics or quotes.
Author Unknown

Purposeful stories - those created with
a specific mission in mind -
are essential in persuading others
to support a vision or cause.
Peter Guber

Ladies and gentlemen once kept commonplace books,
magpie boards containing scraps of literature,
historical facts, bon mots—any bauble that
snagged the owner's fancy—
that were consulted and memorized
before engagements,
lest opportunity arose to flourish them
and impress the company.
Catherine Blyth

Be unpredictable, be real, be interesting.
Tell a good story.
James Dasher

There's a big, wonderful world out there for you.
It belongs to you. It's exciting and stimulating
and rewarding. Don't cheat yourself out of it.
Nancy Reagan

Don't confuse stimulating with being blunt.
Barbara Walters

Be still when you have nothing to say;
when genuine passion moves you,
say what you've got to say,
and say it hot.
D. H. Lawrence

PNF: Being a skillful conversationalist is vital to being a socially successful person. You appear the most interesting to another person when you are interested in *them*. But, to actually *be* interesting, one must cultivate a variety of interests—don't be one-dimensional. Make it your business to be well-informed about current affairs; read at least one newspaper on a daily basis; travel; go to the theater; and never attend a social event without first planning what you might say that would be engaging and interesting to those who will be in attendance. Contrary to what Woody Allen has said—"Eighty percent of success is showing up"—we have to make an effort to be interesting.

Empowering Tips

1 **BE A SKILLFUL SMALL TALKER.** Small talk is the first level of a conversation—before the more interesting or more personal part of the conversation begins. Small talk makes people feel comfortable because it is what you share in common—the weather, the event, etc. Even a smile accompanied by a "Hello" is considered small talk.

2 **DON'T COMPLAIN.** Avoid talking about your problems, since that is the most boring topic of conversation according to research.

3 **DON'T ASK PERSONAL QUESTIONS.** Although you may be interested in how old a person is, whether or not they are married, or how much money they make, you should never ask these questions—unless you want to be considered rude.

4 **FOCUS ON THE OTHER PERSON.** Use the word "you" more than you use the word "I" if you want others to remain interested in talking to you. Lean toward them, make eye contact, and listen intently to them without thinking about what you are going to say when they stop talking. Truly listening to another person is one of the highest compliments you can pay them.

5 **ENTER AND EXIT CONVERSATIONS GRACIOUSLY.** Once you have considerately entered a conversation with another person, always politely excuse yourself as well—never simply melt from conversations. You can say something like, "I have enjoyed talking with you and hearing about XYZ, but if you will please excuse me, I need to…."

Joyful

Joyful: Feeling, expressing or causing
great pleasure and happiness.

People naturally like to be in good spirits,
to laugh, and feel uplifted—and are drawn to those
who make them feel that way.
Ann Demarais and Valerie White

I love people who make me laugh.
I honestly think it's the thing I like most, to laugh.
It cures a multitude of ills.
It's probably the most important thing in a person.
Audrey Hepburn

The world is so full of a number of things
that we should all be happy as kings.
Robert Louis Stevenson

If you want others to be happy, practice compassion.
If you want to be happy, practice compassion.
Dalai Lama

Some cause happiness wherever they go;
others, whenever they go.
Oscar Wilde

Happiness is a choice. You can choose to be happy.
There's going to be stress in life, but it's your
choice whether you let it affect
you or not.
Valerie Bertinelli

Happiness radiates like the fragrance from a flower
and draws all good things toward you.
Maharishi Mahesh

PNF: Give the gift of laughter! One doesn't have to be a comedian. Just being less serious, and directing your attention to the humorous side of things, will make you appear more approachable and fun to be around. Even smiling at another person and paying them a compliment can be uplifting and make them feel good about themselves.

Ellen DeGeneres has a wonderful ability to make people laugh. She *is* a comedian, but a far from average one. She exudes joyfulness. Jerry Seinfeld is another comedian who seems like a genuinely nice and happy person. He makes us laugh without being vulgar—keeping his act "sex-and-swear-free." His Seinfeld episodes have helped us view the humor in, and lighter side of, relationships and embarrassing social situations, rather than seeing the dark side of them. Life doesn't always have to be so serious.

Empowering Tips

1 **LAUGH WHEN SOMEONE TELLS YOU A JOKE**. Even if the joke isn't funny, laugh, unless it is a vulgar or tasteless joke. It's a very gracious thing to do.

2 **USE HUMOR AT THE OFFICE.** Using humor at the office can boost your status, but only if it's the right kind. Humor at work can elevate you to being viewed as confident and competent, according to a recent study by the Wharton School and Harvard. Self-deprecating humor for bosses makes them seem more confident, but also more approachable. Humor relieves stress, can build rapport, and even create more productivity. Joy and laughter can lighten any mood or situation.

3 **LAUGH AT YOURSELF.** If someone laughs at something you've done, laugh with them. It will help relieve your embarrassment and put the others around you at ease. It's a very generous thing to do. Plus, it shows you are resilient when you don't take yourself so seriously and can laugh off a mistake you've made. Everyone makes mistakes. "Just pick yourself up and start all over again." Of course some mistakes call for an "I'm sorry" if you have done or said something to hurt or embarrass another person.

4 **FOLLOW YOUR BLISS.** You may not be able to make your passion or doing what you love your life's work, but you can make it your avocation, devoting your free time to it. Many people have to take jobs they don't like to support their dream of someday doing what they love.

5 **DO ONE JOYFUL THING EACH DAY.** Every day of your life do something, see something, or listen to something that brings you joy—even if it's just for a few minutes. And every day of your life do at least one thing that will bring another person joy. Doing something for another person will bring *you* joy and make you a happier person.

Kind

Kind: Having or showing a friendly,
generous, and considerate nature.

*It is often the small kindnesses—the smiles,
the gestures, compliments, favors—
that can make our day and even change our lives.*
Linda Kaplan Thaler and Robin Koval

*Too often we underestimate the power of a touch,
a listening ear, an honest compliment,
or the smallest act of caring, all of which
have the power to turn a life around.*
Leo F. Buscaglia

*The little remembered acts of kindness and love
are the best parts of a person's life.*
William Wordsworth

*Let us always meet each other with a smile,
for the smile is the beginning of love.*
Mother Teresa

*A young woman should remember
that by making another person feel small,
she only succeeds in diminishing herself.*
Kay West

*We should all consider each other as
human beings, and we should respect each other.*
Malala Yousafzai

Kindness in words creates confidence.
Kindness in thinking creates profoundness.
Kindness in giving creates love.
Lao Tzu

PNF: My mother once said to me: "It doesn't take much effort to be kind. One should always be kind." You will always be judged more by your kindness than by any other trait. Simple things like letting someone in front of you at the grocery store when they have fewer items; holding the elevator door open for a person who is rushing to catch it; or treating a friend, who has recently lost his job, to dinner—these are all acts of kindness that will make you a better, happier person.

Many of our celebrities and sports figures are known and written about for doing kind things for others; but I am certain many of you can cite countless examples of kind acts you have seen performed by everyday people that no one will ever hear about—at least that is my hope.

Empowering Tips

1 **TREAT OTHERS THE WAY YOU WOULD LIKE TO BE TREATED**. Etiquette is the rules for socially-acceptable behavior; manners are how we use the rules of etiquette: treating others with kindness, consideration, and respect. Whenever you are in doubt about what you should do in a particular situation, think of how you would like to be treated and behave in a way that shows your consideration and respect for the people around you.

2 **SMILE TO SHOW WARMTH.** There is nothing like a smile to create a good first impression. A warm and confident smile will put you and the person you are meeting at ease; and besides, it is the polite thing to do. The key to an authentic smile is to think pleasant thoughts. Be mindful of your thoughts when greeting others, and smile when you say their name. It will make you appear genuinely happy to meet *them*.

3 **BE INCLUSIVE**. Being inclusive, rather than exclusive, is especially kind. If you are part of a group conversing at a social event and you see someone standing outside of the group who looks like they might like to join you, invite them to join in. It's a very generous act.

4 **LADIES FIRST.** "After you." Two of the nicest words one can utter to another. Everyone knows that ladies and guests always go first, but why not just let someone go ahead of you for no other reason than it is a nice, selfless thing to do?

5 **RESPECT YOURSELF.** Of course you will be kind to others and show respect for them, but what about yourself? The way you treat yourself is the way others will treat you. When you show respect for yourself, others will respect you as well.

Likeable

Likeable: Having qualities that bring about
a favorable regard: pleasant;
agreeable; personable.

*Likability has something to do with how you look,
but a lot more to do with how you make people feel.
If people like you, they will give you their attention
and happily open up to you.*
Nicholas Boothman

*The art of attracting other people consists of
10% projection of success, 10% appearance,
10% intelligence, and 70% charm.*
David Barton

*I've learned that people will forget what you said,
people will forget what you did,
but people will never forget how you made them feel.*
Maya Angelou

*I've trained myself to illuminate the things
in my personality that are likeable and to
hide and protect the things that are less likeable.*
Will Smith

*For people to like you, they have to accept you.
For people to accept you, you have to accept them.*
Guy Kawasaki

When it comes right down to it,
whatever business you're in,
you're in the people business.
After all, people prefer to do business
with people and companies they find likeable.
Karen Salmansohn

If we want users to like our software,
we should design it to behave like a likeable person.
Alan Cooper

PNF: In order to be likeable, I believe one must genuinely like other people and show an interest in *them*. Charming people are more interested in what the other person has to say than what they themselves have to say; and by showing genuine interest in others, it makes them exceptionally likeable.

Larry King was one of the most well-liked talk show hosts on TV. He was so successful, I believe, because he showed genuine interest in other people and always treated them with respect when he interviewed them. Everyone, in turn, liked him and felt comfortable when they were interviewed by him. Charlie Rose is another person who shows genuine interest in everyone he interviews. He leans in, makes intense eye contact, and listens as if mesmerized as they reveal themselves to him.

Empowering Tips

1 MAKE A POSITIVE FIRST IMPRESSION. Research shows that most people decide whether or not they like you within the first seven seconds of meeting you. First impressions are in great part tied to your body language. Good posture, a firm handshake, a smile, and directly facing the person you are talking to will ensure a positive first impression.

2 LEARN TO BE CHARMING. When conversing with someone, give them your undivided attention. Charm them by making them feel as if they are the most fascinating person in the room. Point your whole body in their direction, and never look around at others.

3 BE SOCIALABLE. Likeable people give clear signals of their willingness to be sociable, primarily by their body language. They generally exude confidence and an easygoing personality. They are welcoming and friendly, and they get other people's attention. If you want others to like you and open up to you, you have to signal you are "open for business" with your smile and warmth. Just as important as being able to approach others, is looking approachable yourself.

4 PUT OTHERS AT EASE. People do business with people they like and with whom they feel comfortable. To get people to like you, show a genuine interest in them and find out what is important to them. It's called building rapport. Build rapport first; get them to like you; then sell them your products or services.

5 REMEMBER NAMES. To quote Dale Carnegie: "A person's name is to that person, the sweetest, most important sound in any language." Likeable people make certain they remember and use others' names every time they see them. If you have trouble remembering names, keep a small notebook with you to write down the name of each new person you meet, with something about them that will help you remember their name.

Magnanimous

Magnanimous: Very generous or forgiving,
especially toward a rival or
someone less powerful than oneself.

*One of the sanest, surest and most generous
joys of life comes from being happy
over the good fortunes of others.*
Robert A. Heinlein

*I propose that as a society we take a new,
close look at that intriguing code of behavior
based on respect, restraint,
and responsibility that we call civility.*
Dr. P.M. Forni

*We don't have to share the same opinions
of others, but we need to be respectful.*
Taylor Swift

*Give people the benefit of the doubt.
Assume people are honest, smart, and decent
—not dishonest, stupid, and conflicted.*
Guy Kawasaki

*Real generosity is doing something nice
for someone who will never find out.*
Frank A. Clark

*Life's most urgent question:
'What are you doing for others?*
Martin Luther King Jr.

Philanthropy is not about the money.
It's about using whatever resources you have
at your fingertips and
applying them to improving the world.
Melinda Gates

PNF: Show appreciation for others. Compliment them. Make them feel good about themselves by listening to them and pointing out their positive qualities. This is how magnanimous, charming, civilized people treat one another. In order to be a person of substance, it is necessary to have a high regard for others, and to do all one can to help those who are less fortunate. Being magnanimous or charitable is as much about thinking kind thoughts of others and treating them kindly as it is about giving them our time, money, or services.

Tyra Banks, a former top model, is a perfect case in point. She is using her genial nature and magnetic personality to mentor girls and young women with her TZONE Foundation. Other female celebrities who get personally involved in their humanitarian causes and giving include Taylor Swift, Lady Gaga, Kristin Stewart, Emma Watson, Anne Hathaway, and Oprah Winfrey. Of course there are numerous other charitable celebrities and well-known people I could name, but these are stellar examples.

Empowering Tips

1 BE A GENEROUS LISTENER. When conversing with another person, be an attentive and active listener. Make eye contact, use facial expressions, give feedback, and point your whole body toward them. Being a generous, active listener will make *you* a wonderful conversationalist and captivating person in the eyes of the person who is actually doing most, if not all, of the talking.

2 FOCUS ON SIMILAR ATTITUDES WITH NEW PEOPLE. When having a conversation with someone you have just met, focus on your similar attitudes, rather than how you are different. Then, should you have a difference of opinion after you have become better acquainted, it will not be the end of your relationship.

3 AGREE TO DISAGREE. When having a conversation with another person with whom you might not agree, listen to their point of view; and if you disagree, calmly and politely present your point of view. If you are unable to come to an agreement, simply agree to disagree. Win-Win is another strategy to employ when you are in disagreement about how to proceed when you have differing points of view. Always let your "opponent" save face. In negotiations, compromise is almost always necessary. When both parties walk away from the table feeling they have gotten something they wanted, there will be fewer hard feelings or resentment about the concessions they made.

4 SHARE THE CREDIT. When you receive praise for a job well done, be generous and share the credit with those who worked with you on the project. It's the right thing to do, and those who helped you will be eager to help you again.

5 GIVE WHATEVER YOU CAN. Time is often more precious than money. If you are unable to give money to a cause, a gift of your time will almost always be welcome. Volunteering is as rewarding to you as it is to the cause you support.

Nice

Nice: Pleasant in manner;
good-natured; kind.

*Nice does not mean smiling blandly
while others walk all over you.
No matter what you are doing,
being nice will make you more successful at it.*
Linda Kaplan Thaler and Robin Koval

*Be nice to people on your way up
because you'll meet then on your way down.*
Wilson Mizner

*Be nice to nerds.
Chances are you will be working for them.*
Bill Gates

*Success can make you go one of two ways.
It can make you a prima donna,
or it can smooth the edges,
take away the insecurities
and let the nice things come out.*
Barbara Walters

*For every rude executive who makes it to
the top, there are nine successful executives
with good manners.*
Letitia Baldrige

*The little remembered acts of kindness
and love are the best parts of a person's life.*
William Wordsworth

*We can improve our relationships
with others by leaps and bounds
if we become encouragers instead of critics.*
Joyce Meyer

PNF: Being nice is the hallmark of a well-bred, well-mannered person. Simple things like saying, "Good morning" to the people you encounter first thing in the morning; holding the door open for someone; or offering to help them pick up something they have dropped, leave an indelible impression.

Tom Hanks, whom all consider the nicest man in Hollywood, treats everyone with respect. Tales of his kindness and humanity abound, as well as his genuine humility and generosity with cast and crew members on the sets of his movies. Nice guys (and gals) can certainly finish first—not last, as you may have heard.

Empowering Tips

PRACTICE NICE MANNERS. Being nice and having good manners includes some of the following considerate acts:

1 Let others exit elevators, buildings and public transportation before you attempt to enter them.

2 Hold the door open for people following closely behind you or for someone who may need a little help entering a building or public transportation.

3 When walking on the sidewalk or riding an escalator, keep to the right so that others can pass on your left.

4 Be mindful of others if you are talking or texting on your cell phone when walking down the street, getting on public transportation, walking up a set of stairs, or going up to a cashier in a store to pay for an item.

5 Give up your seat to someone who may need it more than you—the elderly, a caregiver with small children, a woman who is pregnant, or people on crutches.

Optimism

Optimism: Hopefulness and confidence
about the future or the
successful outcome of something.

*A pessimist sees the difficulty in every opportunity;
an optimist sees the opportunity in every difficulty.*
Winston Churchill

*Our doubts are traitors and make us
lose the ground we might oft win
by fearing to attempt.*
William Shakespeare

*Optimism is the faith that leads to achievement.
Nothing can be done without hope and confidence.*
Helen Keller

*I think it is important to get your surroundings
as well as yourself in a positive state—
meaning surround yourself with positive people,
not the kind who are negative,
and jealous of everything you do.*
Heidi Klum

*Your attitude, not your aptitude,
will determine your altitude.
Positive thinking will let you do everything better
than negative thinking will.*
Zig Ziglar

When you have a passion, and you create things,
and you see people enjoy it,
the money and the business comes second.
Jean-Georges Vongerichten

Success is not the key to happiness.
Happiness is the key to success.
If you love what you are doing,
you will be successful.
Albert Schweitzer

PNF: Decide that you are going to be successful and you will be. Be confident in your ability to get the job done. One of my elementary school teachers used to say to me, "Can't never did anything" when I said I couldn't do something. And to this day, I hear her say it when I start to doubt myself.

Derek Jeter's mother, Dorothy, instilled a positive attitude in him when he was growing up by insisting that he not use the word "can't." He, of course, turned out to be one of the best baseball players of his generation and helped the New York Yankees win five World Series championships.

As Brian Adams said, "Like attracts like. Whatever the conscious mind thinks and believes, the subconscious mind provides." Visualizing your goals is a powerful tool for helping you reach your goals. And in the words of Sheryl Sandberg, "Feeling confident—or pretending that you feel confident—is necessary to reach for opportunities. It's a cliché but opportunities are rarely offered; they're seized."

Empowering Tips

1 BE FUN TO BE AROUND. It is very simple: positive people are more likeable and fun to be around than negative people. Being fun also means being a good sport—not only in sports, but in life. Take your losses with the same good cheer you take your wins; there's always next time.

2 PAY IT FORWARD. Be generous with your support of others. Networking, in particular, is a reciprocal activity. If you have a lead on a job or company that might need the services of someone other than yourself, pass the lead on. Do it, not because you expect them to help you—although they may at some point—but because it is a generous thing to do.

3 COUNT THE COST OF YOUR GOAL. When you set a goal for yourself, calculate the cost to achieve the goal—how much time and resources you will need to commit to it. If the cost is too high, you might want to revise the goal; or consider setting small, achievable goals that will help you reach your final, larger goal.

4 LEARN FROM YOUR MISTAKES. Success or failure in any endeavor depends more than anything else on how you respond to events or circumstances. If something doesn't go as planned, and you did not get the result you expected, think of it as a "teaching moment" and ask yourself what you can do next time to receive a more favorable outcome. Sometimes, "What seems to us as bitter trials are often blessings in disguise," according to Oscar Wilde.

5 EXPECT THE BEST POSSIBLE OUTCOME. Being optimistic doesn't mean sitting back waiting for things to happen by themselves. It means expecting good things to happen, believing they will happen, and taking action to make them happen. More importantly, don't spend your time worrying that they won't happen. Worrying is a waste of your time. It turns optimism into pessimism and you begin to doubt yourself.

Polish

Polish: Refinement or elegance
in a person or thing.

*You don't get a second chance to
make a first impression.*
Author Unknown

*A polished appearance is the filter through
which your leadership and communication skills
are initially evaluated; and no one will bother to assess
your communication skills or your leadership capabilities
if your appearance telegraphs you are clueless.*
Sylvia Di Giusto

*Life is not about finding yourself,
it is about creating yourself.*
Edgar Allen Poe

*I'm becoming more and more myself
with time. I guess that's what grace is,
the refinement of your soul.*
Jewel

*Have the daring to accept yourself
as a bundle of possibilities
and undertake the game
of making the most of your best.*
Harry Emerson Fosdick

I seek constantly to improve my manners
and social graces, for they are the sugar
to which all are attracted.
Og Mandino

The way for a young man to rise
is to improve himself in every way he can,
never suspecting that anybody wished
to hinder him.
Abraham Lincoln

PNF: Learning to project a polished and positive image is paramount to success. A polished appearance opens doors! Your personal polishing is simply a matter of learning and applying the rules of socially-acceptable behavior; knowing how to dress in a way that it not only appropriate, but stylish and personally enhancing; and always, always being well groomed.

To be polished, you must make the extra effort to see that everything you do is as perfect as it can be. Polishing a speech; double-checking an email to ensure that there are no typos; never leaving the house with unpolished shoes or wrinkled clothes; maintaining good posture; cultivating an accent-free voice; and making sure that your digital imprint is just as polished as your offline and in-person image.

Empowering Tips

POLISH YOUR TABLE MANNERS. Not only does it make it more pleasant for those with whom you are dining when you have polished table manners, but it also shows consideration for them. The table is the ultimate proving ground for making a positive impression on your friends, coworkers, boss, and current or future in-laws.

1 LEARN HOW TO READ A TABLE SETTING. Your bread plate is to the left of your dinner plate and your glass is to the right of it. Think BMW: bread, main course, water. You will know how many courses you are going to have and in which order they will be served by looking at the utensils at your place setting. For example, since utensils are used from the outside in, if your salad fork is the outermost utensil to the left of your plate, it tells you that a salad will be served before the main course.

2 KNOW HOW TO PROPERLY HOLD AND USE YOUR CUTLERY. There are two styles of dining when eating with knives and forks: the American style and the Continental, or European, style. The way you hold your utensils, as well as the cutting position, is the same for both styles. How you use them to eat and place them on the plate to indicate you are "resting" or finished is done differently for each style. Make it a point to master silverware savvy if you want to be viewed favorably at the table.

3 USE YOUR NAPKIN CORRECTLY. Learn how to fold your napkin to place it on your lap; use the napkin as needed to gently dab, not wipe, the corners of your mouth. Never place a used napkin back on the table until the host or hostess signals that the meal is over by placing his or her napkin on the table, and everyone is ready to depart from the table.

4 REMEMBER YOUR DINING ETIQUETTE. Wait to begin eating until everyone at the table has been served if you are with a small group, or until your host has given the signal by picking up his or her knife and fork. Chew quietly with your mouth closed and swallow your food before talking. Cut and eat one piece of meat at a time. Break your bread and spread the butter on one small piece at time. Avoid unpleasant or controversial topics at the table.

5 **BUILD RAPPORT WITH YOUR DINNER COMPANIONS**. When you are dining out with other people, order the same number of courses and eat at the same pace. If you are at a business function or having an interview luncheon, it is best that you only order manageable foods that can be eaten with a knife and fork. This leaves you free to build rapport and get to know the person with whom you are dining, which is the main purpose of business meals.

*Q*uality

Quality: General excellence
of standard or level.

Be a yardstick of quality.
Some people aren't used to an environment
where excellence is expected.
Steve Jobs

Try not to become a man of success
but rather to become a man of value.
Albert Einstein

Leaders relentlessly upgrade their team,
using every encounter as an opportunity
to evaluate, coach, and build self-confidence.
Jack Welch

A mode of conduct, a standard of courage,
discipline, fortitude, and integrity
can do a great deal to make a woman beautiful.
Jacqueline Bisset

The greatness of art is not to find what is
common but what is unique.
Issac Bashevis Singer

There is nothing noble in being superior to
your fellow man. True nobility lies in being
superior to your former self.
Ernest Hemingway

The quality of a person's life
is in direct proportion to their
commitment to excellence,
regardless of their chosen field of endeavor.
Vince Lombardi

PNF: Never sacrifice quality to quantity. Always buy the best accessories you can afford. Shoes, belts and bags say more about your personal style than anything you can wear on your back. And when you invest in yourself, others will want to invest in you; they will take you at your own self-worth.

More importantly, *be* a person of quality, and a role model to all who know you, depend upon you, or look up to you. Sports figures are among the most widely watched and emulated people. Some athletes who make exemplary role models include Serena Williams, Tim Tebow, Amy Purdy, Jimmie Johnson, Rory McIlroy, and Russell Wilson. All are great athletes who have demonstrated by their hard work, devotion to their sport, attitude, and generosity that they deserve our respect and are the kind of people to aspire to be.

Empowering Tips

1 BE YOUR OWN GREAT, UNIQUE SELF. You can decide to be average and like everyone else, or you can decide to become your own person and be great. Certainly as a teenager it is much easier to be like everyone else and fit in. It takes courage to be your own person. Nevertheless, you can decide that you will always put forth your best effort, never settling for average when you can be, or make, something great.

2 SET THE BAR HIGH. Develop your leadership skills. Be a role model and set the standard for your team. Welcome their input and acknowledge their ideas for how things might be done differently. When you include the team in the planning process, they will always feel more invested in making it happen.

3 EXCEED EXPECTATIONS. Sometimes all others will demand of you is that you do an adequate job. Perhaps it is all they think you are capable of doing. When you exceed their expectations, not only will you raise their opinion of your capabilities and you as a person; but exceeding the expectations of others will give you a sense of pride in yourself and elevate your self-esteem.

4 PROVIDE SUPERIOR SERVICE. Many brick-and-mortar and online stores offer the same or similar products. Why do we buy from one versus another, assuming price is the same at each? It is the quality of their service and how they make us feel when we are shopping in their store or on their website. Like stores and companies, we are marketing ourselves to our consumers or clients. How do you differentiate yourself? Do you offer superior service or just average service?

5 SEEK INSPIRATION. Surround yourself with great people, great ideas, great literature, and with people who love, support, and inspire you to greatness. If there is someone you aspire to be like, ask that person to be your mentor. If that is not possible, read everything you can about a person who inspires you, and use the person as an example for how to live your life to achieve greatness.

Rapport

Rapport: A relationship characterized by agreement, mutual understanding, or empathy that makes communication possible or easy.

Rapport is the ability to connect with others in a positive way. Its essential component is YOU and the courtesy and empathy you show others.
Nicholas Boothman

Rapport is that feeling of being comfortable with someone and trusting them. It's my experience that people do business with people they know, like and trust.
Tracey Dowe

For women, the language of conversation is primarily a language of rapport: a way of establishing connections and negotiating relationships.
Deborah Tannen

When you start to develop your powers of empathy and imagination the whole world opens up to you.
Susan Sarandon

You have no credibility if you don't apply
mirroring and matching skills to
your communication.
Mirroring and matching communicates
a level of understanding
and empathy of that person's world.
Page Haviland, Ph.D.

Use anything you can think of to
understand and be understood, and you'll
discover the creativity
that connects you with others.
Martha Beck

When you find your passion, it's great.
You go up to a mountain with partners,
and you have a wonderful opportunity to connect
and achieve good together.
You are not trying to be better than other humans.
You are supporting each other.
Conrad Anker

PNF: People like, and feel comfortable with, people like themselves. For communication to be effective there needs to be rapport or a mutual understanding. You build rapport by making the other person feel that you understand them or that you have something in common with them. Begin with small talk to determine what you have in common, and establish a rapport before you try to sell your service or product.

Oprah Winfrey seems to have a natural affinity with people from all walks of life. This seemingly innate skill, along with her impressive business skills, has made her one of the most successful women in the world today.

Empowering Tips

1 MAKE POSITIVE CONNECTIONS. Having rapport with another person means that we connect with them in a positive way— that we feel comfortable with them; and understood by them. We have a natural rapport with people with whom we have things in common, such as background, interests, religion, or political party; but you can learn to build instant rapport with people you have just met.

2 BUILD RAPPORT DURING INTRODUCTIONS. Show respect for the person to whom you are being introduced by making eye contact, facing them directly, and giving them a firm handshake as you state your greeting: "Hello, Charlotte, it is such a pleasure to meet you." If you are meeting a more senior person or VIP, you should use their honorific along with their last name: "Hello, Ms. Smith, it is an honor to meet you."

3 BE EMPATHETIC. Put yourself in the other person's shoes and see the world from their point of view. Only when you do this can you truly understand them. Everyone likes to feel heard and understood. And when someone feels understood, they feel rapport with you.

4 MIRROR AND MATCH. Act in a similar manner to the person to whom you're talking. Mirroring the other person's body language, stance, how they handle information, the speed and volume of their speech, their choice of words, etc., helps build rapport.

5 DRESS TO FIT IN. Another way to build rapport with others is to dress the way they dress. It's why you are always advised to dress as if you already work for the company to which you are going for an interview. It's why people who are in the same social circle often dress alike. Dressing similarly signals you are members of the same tribe. The clothes you wear are the outward expression of your personality and who you are inside.

Style

Style: Distinction and elegance of manner and bearing.

*The goal I seek is to have people refine
their style through my clothing without having
them become victims of fashion.*
Giorgio Armani

*I don't believe in changing my style
because something's a trend.
People are misled: They think because
something's a trend, they should do it.
And it's not going to work.*
Rachael Zoe

*I appreciate individuality.
Style is much more interesting than fashion, really.*
Marc Jacobs

*The zenith of elegance in any woman's wardrobe
is the little black dress,
the power of which suggests dash and elegance.*
Andre Leon Talley

*Fashion is about dressing according
to what's fashionable.
Style is more about being yourself.*
Oscar de la Renta

*I think all girls in the world wish
they were a Parisian girl—that sort of
effortless chic, confidence and comfort
in their own skin.*
Natalie Portman

*I've always loved fashion because
it's a great way to express your mood.
A woman can wear confidence
on her feet with a high stiletto,
or slip into weekend comfort
with a soft ballet flat.*
Fergie

PNF: No matter what fashion happens to dictate for accessories each season, I always wear pearls. They're part of my personal style. Perhaps you're known for your Manolo Blahnik's, designer handbags, signature scent, or long blond hair. Or, perhaps you always wear scarves or red lipstick. Whether you realize it or not, your personal style defines you. Actress Natalie Wood's diamond drop earrings were such an important part of her personal style that her daughter insisted she be buried in them.

Classic style icons that immediately come to mind are Grace Kelly, Jacqueline Kennedy, Audrey Hepburn and Katherine Hepburn—each managed to make stylish, ladylike elegance seem effortless and timeless. Today, we have Amal Cloony and Ines de la Fressange, who have that natural glamour and good taste so seemingly common in European women. And I particularly like the Duchess of Cambridge, who exudes a classy, contemporary 'princess' style that has inspired young women everywhere to consider that dressing tastefully can be more attractive than dressing like a Kardashian. Emma Stone, a very likeable young actress, is also showing us that it's possible to turn heads without being ostentatious, wearing tasteful, stylish clothes.

Empowering Tips

1 **WEAR CLOTHES THAT LOOK LIKE THEY WERE MADE FOR YOU.** Dress for your body type or bodyline (the combination of your face shape and body shape). When your clothes look like they were made for you, you will look your best no matter what your size or shape. Keep in mind that, with your particular size or shape, you may not be able to wear every fashion trend that appears. Stay with styles that suit you and you will always look *your* stylish best.

2 **CREATE A UNIQUE PERSONAL STYLE.** Your unique personal style should suit your personality as well as your personal and professional goals. You may need to have a slightly different style for work than you do for weekends, but there should be some consistency; and you should certainly present a consistent image at work. A unique personal style can set you apart and make you more memorable.

3 **A LITTLE PIZZAZZ GOES A LONG WAY.** Today, all a woman needs to do to be fashionable is put on red lipstick, statement earrings, fabulous shoes, a wonderful smile, and she can wear just about anything she chooses—as long as it's appropriate for the occasion. François Nars says, "A fresh face with a red lipstick is timeless. It's supermodern and relaxed but very chic."

4 **KNOW WHAT YOUR STYLE IS SIGNALING ABOUT YOU.** Your personal style conveys instant silent signals about you to others. It behooves you to know what signals you are sending. There are seven universal styles for women and men, according to Alyce Parsons in her book *Style Source: The Power of the Seven Universal Styles for Women and Men.* Determine which of the seven styles is yours to see if it accurately represents you, and projects the signals you intend to send. You just might need to change your style to achieve your goals.

5 **WHEN IN DOUBT, DON'T WEAR IT.** Elegance is achieved through balance and simplicity. If you go overboard with your accessories and focal points, you can appear flashy or, worse, tacky. Although less can sometimes be more, wearing too few or no accessories at all can result in a dull or uninteresting look. As a rule of thumb, three points of interest are the maximum, although less may work better for a particular outfit or occasion. If in doubt, don't wear it.

Thanks

Thanks: An expression of gratitude,
appreciation, or acknowledgment.

Appreciation is a wonderful thing.
It makes what is excellent in others
belong to us as well.
Voltaire

Feeling gratitude and not expressing it
is like wrapping a present and not giving it.
William Ward

As we express our gratitude,
we must never forget that the highest appreciation
is not to utter the words, but to live by them.
John F. Kennedy

Gratitude is a mark of a noble soul and refined character.
We like to be around those who are grateful.
Joseph B. Wirthlin

A compliment is a gift, not to be
thrown away carelessly
unless you want to hurt the giver.
Eleanor Hamilton

Make is a habit to tell people thank you—
to express your appreciation sincerely,
and without the expectation
of anything in return.
Ralph Marston

An engraved or printed thank-you card,
no matter how attractive its design,
cannot take the place of a
personally written message of thanks.
Emily Post

PNF: A hand-written note is elegance personified. Investing in a fine writing pen and personalized stationery will make it a pleasure to write your notes of heartfelt thanks. "Thank you"—two of the most important and gracious words one can utter. Whenever anyone does anything for us, we should thank them—it completes the circle of giving and receiving. Diana, Princess of Wales, always took the time to write a thank-you note to someone who had done something for her, no matter how small the effort or service might have seemed to others. She was the definition of a kind and gracious person.

Empowering Tips

1 **WRITE A THANK-YOU NOTE.** Thanking people is our way of respecting them by showing appreciation. Thank-you notes should be sent to thank someone for sending you a gift, having you as a guest in their home, a meal, or for any special favor. And, of course, a thank-you note should be sent after an interview. All that is needed are a few warm and thoughtfully-stated sentences to show your appreciation.

2 **ALWAYS TAKE A HOSTESS GIFT TO A DINNER PARTY.** Never go empty handed to a dinner party. If you take a bottle of wine, don't expect your host to open it that evening. It is inconsiderate to take fresh flowers because your host, who will be busy with the dinner and her guests, will have to take time away from them to find a vase and put the flowers in water. You may however send fresh flowers with a note the day after the dinner party.

3 **GIVE AN APPROPRIATE RESPONSE.** Any time someone does something for you, a gracious "Thank-you" should be said. When someone thanks you, an appropriate response would be, "You're welcome" or "It was my pleasure." Avoid responding with "No problem," since it actually implies the opposite.

4 **ALWAYS R.S.V.P. TO INVITATIONS.** When you receive an invitation, you should respond to it. It is very rude not to. A timely response is just as important if you are not planning to attend an event as it is if you are planning to attend.

5 **PRACTICE GRATITUDE.** Being thankful for all that you have and practicing gratitude will make you a happier person. When you start thinking about all of the things you don't have—whether it be material possessions or personal attributes—start counting your blessings and you will find you have much to be thankful for.

*U*ndauntable

Undauntable: Not to be deterred or discouraged;
fearless; intrepid.

*I am always doing that which I cannot do,
in order that I may learn to do it.*
Pablo Picasso

*Don't ever let a soul in the world tell you
that you can't be exactly who you are.*
Lady Gaga

*Whether you think you can or whether you
think you can't, you're right.*
Henry Ford

*I have a lot of things to prove to myself.
One is that I can live my life fearlessly.*
Oprah Winfrey

*Not everything that is faced can be changed,
but nothing can be changed until it is faced.*
Franklin Delano Roosevelt

*He who is not courageous enough
to take risks will accomplish nothing in life.*
Muhammad Ali

You really have to be courageous
about your instincts and your ideas.
Otherwise you'll just knuckle under, and things
that might have been memorable will be lost.
Francis Ford Coppola

PNF: There is nothing more infectious than a can-do attitude. Enthusiasm and a fearless approach to life's challenges will make others want to follow you. There is a better person inside of each of us. Our task is to uncover it and do whatever it takes to be that better, self-confident self. When Tommy Hilfiger began his design business at the age of 24, he said "I didn't know anything about design; I just knew I could do it better."

Empowering Tips

1 DON'T BE A WALL FLOWER. When you are invited to a social event, don't let your shyness prevent you from enjoying yourself; and don't let it prevent you from making important connections at a business function. Make an effort; come prepared with something to contribute; take the initiative and introduce yourself to people you don't know and make polite conversation with them.

2 THINK "I'M EXCITED;" NOT, "I'M NERVOUS." When we are nervous about meeting new people or making a presentation, it usually means we are too focused on ourselves and our performance, rather than on the people we are meeting or the audience's needs. Think "I am excited to attend this event or make this presentation," rather than "I am nervous." According to Amy Cuddy, a social psychologist at Harvard, you can change your mindset. "Fake it until you become it," Ms. Cuddy advises.

3 BE FEARLESS. Say to yourself, "I can do it." Take five deep breaths—yes five, not one—calm yourself and carry on. There are times when fear can help us avoid making serious mistakes; but often fear prevents us from accomplishing all that we might otherwise achieve.

4 YOU ARE MORE POWERFUL THAN YOU KNOW. There is nothing like doing or achieving something you did not think was possible. Remember one way to gain confidence is by leaving your comfort zone. Challenge yourself. What could you attempt to do that would bring you a sense of pride if you thought it were even remotely possible? Then, set out to do it. It can be exhilarating!

5 BELIEVE IN YOURSELF. You are your own boss. Take charge of your life. It's fine to get advice from your friends and loved ones, but in the end, only you can decide what is right for you. Don't let anyone stop you from being the person you aspire to be.

Versatile

Versatile: Embracing a variety of subjects,
fields, or skills; turning with ease
from one thing to another.

Whatever it takes for me to win, I'm down for it.
Versatility goes a long way.
The person who is most versatile
has more going for him
than a guy who just does one thing.
Barbara Morgan

I am very versatile.
I'm able to adapt to an environment
and the way I view things based on who I'm with.
Jake T. Austin

The idea of recognizing your strengths
and using them in as versatile a way as you can
is cool to me.
Frank Ocean

The more versatile you make yourself,
the more work you get.
Training makes you more versatile
and ultimately gets you more work.
Julliard taught me that.
Ving Rhames

I think team sports probably teach you
more about giving—
about being unselfish and being flexible.
Chris Evert

Individuals, too, who cultivate a variety of skills,
seem brighter, more energetic and
more adaptable than those who only
know how to do one thing.
Robert Shea

When you're curious,
you find lots of interesting things to do.
Walt Disney

PNF: In order to be interesting, it helps to be multifaceted and accomplished in more than one area, as well as conversant in a number of subjects, such as sports, the arts, current events. A client once told me that she is certain she landed a job with a top investment firm because of her knowledge of fine wines—an interest that wasn't necessary to do her job, but one that would make her an interesting and helpful dinner companion when her firm entertained clients. Broaden your horizons and you will not only be more interesting to others, but you might surprise yourself by how interesting you find the world outside of your *own* world.

Empowering Tips

1 **SING FOR YOUR SUPPER.** When you are invited to a business meal or dinner party, seek to entertain, not be entertained. Do laugh, but not so loudly that you draw attention to yourself; talk to the people on either side of you, but don't monopolize one or the other; avoid talking over the person next to you to talk with someone else; don't talk to those sitting too far away from you if you have to raise your voice to do so; and try to include in your conversations those who don't appear to have anyone to talk to. If you are a charming and polite guest, you will receive more invitations.

2 **EMBRACE DIVERSITY.** In our modern world, we will encounter people who are different from us. When you embrace diversity and treat others as you would like to be treated and try to learn from them, you will expand your universe. Being the leader of a team means making the most of each person's talents to ensure a successful outcome. We are all cogs in the wheel!

3 **DON'T LIMIT YOURSELF TO ONE TOPIC.** Any topic to the exclusion of all others is considered boring. Do not be that person who goes on and on about the same subject all the time, then wonder why everyone avoids you at the next event. If you want to be considered fascinating and have others look forward to speaking with you at events, you need to be able to converse about a number of topics.

4 **READ THE NEWS.** As a citizen of the world, it is your duty to know what is going on in it. When you show interest in the world around you, it makes you appear more interesting to others. Choose a news source that you can go to each day to keep you informed of world affairs. If you think you don't have time, think again. Everyone has five or ten minutes a day to spare. There are many news sources now that give you highlights of the day's news without having to spend a lot of time reading or watching the news. *The Daily Skimm* is a great source for young people; *Google* and *Yahoo* both have one-page recaps of the news, as do all the major networks.

5 TAKE CLASSES TO EXPAND YOUR UNIVERSE. Consider taking a class in a subject that interests you, but that you don't know much about; one that would surprise those who know you. Taking classes is a great way to expand your universe and meet new people. And, it will not only make you appear more interesting to your friends and coworkers; it might even make you feel more positive about yourself.

Well-spoken

Well-spoken: Speaking in an educated,
refined, and courteous manner.

*Your voice is 38% of a first impression;
it is a talking picture of you.
Nothing you can do for your image will
help you as much as improving the way you sound will;
nothing can do more damage, more unjustly,
than a negative response to the way you sound.*
Jeffrey Jacobi

*Your voice is your key communication tool:
and it speaks volumes about who you are
and how the world sees you.
The way you speak is often more important
than your experience, intelligence, education,
appearance, or personality.*
Joni Wilson

*Everything about you speaks—
not just the words you choose
to express your thoughts.
You have five message givers:
the tone of your voice, your eyes,
your face, your bearing, and your dress.*
Dorothy Sarnoff

*There are few words more elementary
or more welcomed than please and thank you.*
Kate Spade

First, communication is not so much
what you say but rather how you say it.
And this you can condition and control.
The tone of your voice; your choice and use of words;
your inflection; articulation; and delivery; and
body language determine how much your listeners
take in—and what overall impression of you
they will form and retain as a result.
Sylvania Ann Hewlett

A gentleman is able to express himself
with a vocabulary larger than four-letter words.
Doris Wood

Be polite in your speeches.
Good information rudely communicated
will make no positive difference.
Israelmore Ayivor

PNF: Not only should your voice sound pleasant, but you must also use good grammar, have a fairly extensive vocabulary, articulate clearly, avoid using filler words, and use thoughtful and considerate words to be considered well spoken.

One of the most articulate men I ever heard speak was William F. Buckley. He was the personification of a well-spoken person. Another person who made a memorable impression on me when I was a child was Richard Burton. Apparently I wasn't the only one, because one time when he was being interviewed on TV, he was given a telephone book and asked to read the names in it. His voice was so appealing that it didn't matter what he said; everyone listened. And then there was Carey Grant, whose voice made women melt. The voice is a powerful element in personal appeal. Make sure the sound of yours will draw others to you.

Empowering Tips

1 DO NOT USE FILLER WORDS. Filler words, such as like, you know, basically, well, uh, etc. detract from the positive impression you make on others, and undermine your credibility in the professional arena. You also want to avoid sloppy words, such as yeah instead of yes, and nah instead of no.

2 BE CIVIL AND TOLERANT. "Let's agree to disagree" and still be friends. Be civil to those whose opinions differ from yours. Name-calling and personal insults are unacceptable and quite rude. Be diplomatic and avoid discussing controversial issues, such as religion or politics, when you are with a group of people with diverse opinions. When you are with like-minded people, sometimes it's okay to discuss controversial issues—as long as you cannot be overheard by those who might be offended by your discussion.

3 SAY I'M SORRY. A simple apology can work magic. If you have done something—intentionally or unintentionally—that offends or upsets another person, apologize. Saying "I'm sorry" works to defuse a situation or soothe hurt feelings.

4 PUT SOME EXPRESSION INTO YOUR VOICE. If you speak in a monotone, you will not attract many listeners. If your voice lacks passion or enthusiasm, it will detract from your message. If you aren't excited about your subject or your life, why should anyone else be? Improving your vocal variety will enhance the power of what you say.

5 MODIFY A STRONG REGIONAL ACCENT. A strong regional accent can stand in the way of getting a job, mixing successfully in social situations, even attracting a mate. If your speech is working against you, taking elocution lessons with a voice coach could help.

Xanadu

Xanadu: An idealized place of great or
idyllic magnificence and beauty.

*Imagine all the people living in peace.
You may say I'm a dreamer,
but I'm not the only one.
I hope someday you'll join us,
and the world will be as one.*
John Lennon

*Music makes life meaningful
because it is about truth and being part
of something bigger than yourself.*
Joshua Bell

*You paint the picture.
Paint it beautifully.*
A.D. Posey

*Life doesn't have to be ordinary.
Why be utilitarian when
you can be exuberant?*
Ken Fulk

*Look up from what you're doing
and look around for a minute.
See what a beautiful world you are in.*
Ralph Marston

*There's a big, wonderful world
out there for you. It belongs to you.
It's exciting and stimulating and rewarding.
Don't cheat yourself out of this promise.*
Nancy Reagan

*If we could make our house a home,
and then make it a sanctuary,
I think we could truly find paradise on Earth.*
Alexandra Stoddard

PNF: Let us make our lives idyllic like Xanadu—it makes for a powerful attraction. Create a beautiful aura: surround yourself with beauty, play beautiful music, have fresh flowers and scented candles in your room, think pleasant thoughts, and you will attract all that is beautiful. I often play Chopin or Mozart when I'm working; and when I am in the mood for something more exhilarating, I play a Pavarotti CD. In the evening, I listen to Frank Sinatra and other artists who sing Cole Porter songs. I always have white orchids for their simplicity and the fact that they can work with any décor.

Music can transport us to a higher, more beautiful place; and it can touch us in ways that words cannot. I once heard Pavarotti say, "I think a life in music is a life beautifully spent, and this is what I have devoted my life to." Can you imagine living in Xanadu for most of your life? I believe Pavarotti felt he did.

Empowering Tips

1 CREATE A CAPTIVATING AMBIENCE. Make your home your own private Xanadu. Create a warm and welcoming environment that greets you at the end of the day—one that makes you happy when you open the door; a home that is a respite from an often less than idyllic world.

2 BE A CHARMING HOST/HOSTESS. When friends or family come to visit you, greet them at the door, take their coat, and offer them something to drink. Create an atmosphere that makes them feel as if they are entering a special world in which they can relax and enjoy themselves. Have fresh flowers, play their favorite kind of music, and offer them treats you know they will like. When you make an effort for others, it makes them feel special and valued.

3 ATTEND CULTURAL EVENTS. The arts can transport and elevate us to a higher plane, and bring us closer to the divine. Visiting an art museum, attending an opera or concert, going to the ballet, or going to see a Broadway play can not only be uplifting, it is an essential part of educating yourself if you want to be considered a cultured person.

4 REINVIGORATE YOURSELF. Jane McGonigal has some wonderful advice in her book *Super Better* for how you can temporarily 'leave' your world to do something that will invigorate you. Some tips she offers include: Go outside and let the sun touch your skin for at least five minutes; stop whatever you are doing and dance to a favorite song; read one of your favorite poems or quotations out loud; and give yourself a hug while telling your body what a great job it is doing.

5 VISIT A MAGICAL PLACE. Plan a trip to a place you've always dreamed of visiting. If time and money won't allow you to do this, take a video tour. Close your eyes and envision yourself there.

Youthful

Youthful: Young or seeming young.

So curiosity, I think, is a really important
aspect of staying young or youthful.
Goldie Hawn

To find joy in work is to discover
the fountain of youth.
Pearl S. Buck

The secret of staying young is to
live honestly, eat slowly, and
to lie about your age.
Lucille Ball

Age is something only in your head
or a stereotype. Age means nothing when
you are passionate about something.
Carolina Herrera

This idea that being youthful is the
only thing that's beautiful or attractive
simply isn't true. I don't want to be an
ageless beauty. I want to be a woman
who is the best I can be at my own age.
Sharon Stone

Age and size are only numbers.
It's the attitude you
bring to clothes that matters.
Donna Karan

Your youth is certainly finished and old age has definitely arrived if you feel you are losing enthusiasm, excitement, and energy towards your dreams.
Amit Kalantri

Yoga is not just a workout, it is a natural way of enhancing flexibility, calmness, clarity, and youthfulness.
Debasish Mridha

PNF: A few years ago my lifelong best friend, Cathy, gave me the book *How Not to Look Old* by Charla Krupp for my birthday. I wasn't sure whether I should be grateful to her or feel insulted. I suppose I felt a little of both. We are the same age and have both been on an endless quest not to look old. I partially blame our mothers and society for making us feel that being – and certainly looking — old is a bad thing. Of course, looking youthful is important for women in most fields today because it keeps them competitive and able to work and provide financial security for themselves. Perception is reality. When we look younger, we signal to others that we are up to the task; that we have the energy, enthusiasm and drive to be successful for ourselves and the company we represent.

So yes, it is important to stay as youthful and young looking as we can. But this includes much more than our looks; it includes our health, vitality, spirit, contribution to society, and outlook on life. Christie Brinkley and Sara Jessica Parker are two wonderful examples of youthful aging.

Empowering Tips

1 PRACTICE MINDFULNESS. Mindfulness is the practice of purposely focusing attention on the present moment and accepting it without judgment. Practicing mindfulness, or meditation, will improve your overall well-being, happiness, and physical and mental health—all of which will make you more youthful. It can be done at any time during the day when you want to become fully engaged in what you are doing. All you need to do is focus on your breathing and staying in the moment.

2 TAKE YOGA AND GET REGULAR CARDIOVASCULAR EXERCISE. For young and old alike, nothing will ensure that you stay youthful longer than exercise. It is good for your mind, body, and soul; and it is a very good stress reliever. There are many new theories about how much time and effort you need to put into exercise to make it most efficient. Do your research and find the exercise program that suits you. Yoga is recommended because, among other things, it keeps you flexible.

3 EAT HEALTHFUL FOODS. To maximize longevity and mental performance, eat nutritiously. Although genes play a role in aging, in most cases your lifestyle and diet play an even larger role. According to research, diet exerts the most profound and lasting effect on keeping us healthy and preventing us from premature aging and decline. Along with eating healthfully, be sure to drink enough water. Among the many benefits it provides, water helps keeps your skin from looking dry and wrinkled, both of which make you look older.

4 GET ENOUGH QUALITY SLEEP. Sleep is regenerating. It is essential for your health and well-being and staying young. Among the many things sleep does for you, it plays a role in regulating moods and reducing stress. When it's time for bed, turn off your television, cell phone and other electronic devices; drink some caffeine-free herbal tea or hot milk; try not to think about your problems; close your eyes; do Dr. Andrew Weil's 4-7-8 breathing exercise. You just might be able to get to sleep faster and stay asleep longer naturally.

5 **AVOID OBVIOUS AGE GIVEAWAYS.** When you get older, more than likely you will need to change the way you wear your hair and apply your makeup. A dated hairstyle can add years to your appearance, and putting on too much or the wrong kind of makeup can make you look older rather than younger. Wearing the same clothing style as your daughter or wearing ill-fitting or out-of-date fashions will also age you. When you dress for your age and personal style, and wear figure-flattering clothes in colors that are right for your skin tone, you will look more youthful.

Zeal

Zeal: Great energy or enthusiasm in pursuit of a cause or an objective.

Passion is energy.
Feel the power that comes
from focusing on what excites you.
Oprah Winfrey

We are perfectionists.
We are hungry to work all the time.
We are entertained by every aspect of business
and never want to stop working.
Suzy Welch

Everything I do in life
is a matter of heart,
body and soul.
Donna Karan

Work hard.
Laugh when you feel like crying.
Keep an open mind, and an open spirit.
Rachel Ray

Success is the ability to go from
one failure to another
with no loss of enthusiasm.
Winston Churchill

Enthusiasm is the greatest asset
you can possess, for it can take you
further than money, power or influence.
Dada Vaswani

There isn't any great mystery about me.
What I do is glamorous and has an
awful lot of white-hot attention placed on it.
But the actual work requires the same discipline
and passion as any job you love doing,
be it as a very good pipe fitter or a highly creative artist.
Tom Hanks

PNF: Whatever we pursue in life, let us pursue it with zeal. Nothing attracts others like enthusiasm; nothing enriches our lives more than eagerly pursuing our dreams; and nothing brings more happiness, in my opinion, than working toward a worthwhile goal and achieving it. I love what I do. I have always been interested in self-improvement and being the best I can be, and helping others to be their personal best. I meet with people from all over the world and, while I am instructing them, I, in turn, always learn something interesting as well. What they say is true: When you love what you do and look forward to each day, it never seems like work; and your genuine enthusiasm will be evident to your colleagues and clients.

Empowering Tips

1 DON'T BE AFRAID TO MAKE MISTAKES. Sometimes we only discover what we want to do by trying something. Focus on what you think you want to do, and work very hard to make it happen. If it wasn't meant to be, or you realize it isn't something you want after all, that's okay. You've heard the expression: "Nothing ventured, nothing gained." It's very true.

2 BE TENACIOUS. Pursue your dreams with all of your resources. Don't let others tell you that you can't do something. Only you can decide that. If you have tried your best to make it happen, and it doesn't, it probably wasn't meant to be.

3 PURSUE YOUR LIFE WITH PASSION. When you are passionate about what you do you will attract others to you. Nothing is as attractive to others as a person who thrives on what they do. Nothing will make you feel more energized than passionately pursuing what you love.

4 LIVE A MEANINGFUL LIFE. Determine what gives you meaning in your life and devote as much time as you can to it. You only have one life to live; when you live it with a sense of purpose, you will feel more fulfilled.

5 BE HERE NOW. Make every day count. Plan for the future, but live in the moment. Be fully present, since only by living in the moment can you enjoy life to the fullest as you pursue your dreams with zeal.

Personal Action Plan

I recommend you focus on one quality or attribute (A, B, C) a week, or one a month, and concentrate on it until you have mastered it. Then go on to the next one. You have as long as it takes. You are only competing against yourself.

I. Make a master plan for yourself.
What would you like to be?

_____

_____

What would you like to do with your life?

_____

_____

What would you like to achieve with your career?

_____

_____

What would you like to achieve in your personal life?

_____

_____

What would you like to be known for by your friends, family, colleagues?

_____

_____

II. Take stock of yourself.

What 4 words best describe you?

_____   _____

_____   _____

List 4 improvements you need to make to be more successful in your personal life.

_____   _____

_____   _____

List 4 improvements you need to make to be more successful in your professional life.

_____   _____

_____   _____

Do you already have what you need (skills, knowledge, etc.) to accomplish your goals?
Yes_____   No_____   Explain_____

_____

_____

Do you need to take some classes, gain some new skills, lose weight, buy a new wardrobe, etc. to achieve your goals? If so, explain.

_____

_____

_____

III. Write an Action Plan with specific goals and a timetable for accomplishing them.
Make three headings: 1. Goals 2. Date to be Accomplished 3. Date Accomplished

IV. Write a personal brand statement.

_____

_____

_____

V. Buy a journal to record your thoughts during the process of your transformation.

Self-Presentation Questionnaire

*Answer Yes or No**

1. Do you think you make a good first impression?

2. Do you enter a room confidently with your head held high?

3. Are you at ease in social situations?

4. Do you know how to make proper introductions?

5. Do you shake hands with confidence?

6. Do you make the appropriate amount of eye contact when you meet and listen to others?

7. Do you know how to initiate conversations with new people?

8. Do you have a pleasant-sounding voice?

9. Do you speak without using fillers and sloppy words?

10. Do you know what the way you dress says about you?

11. Do you always make sure you are well groomed?

12. Do you wear clothes that fit properly and are flattering to your figure.

13. Do you know what your attitude and body language say about you?

14. Are you confident that your dining skills and table manners make a good impression?

15. Are you usually offered a job when you go for an interview?

---

* The answer to every question should be "yes." If it isn't, you have work to do to turn each "no" into a "yes."

Ideas and Inspiration

Glossary of People Quoted

Ali, Muhammad, Professional boxer-activist
Angelou, Maya, Poet-memoirist-activist
Anker, Conrad, Rock climber
Aristotle, Philosopher
Armani, Giorgio, Fashion designer
Austin, Jake T., Actor
Ayivor, Israelmore, Leadership coach-entrepreneur-author
Bach, Johann Sebastian, Composer
Baldrige, Letitia, Author-etiquette expert
Ball Lucille, Actress-comedian-producer
Barton, David, Fitness guru-entrepreneur
Beck, Martha, Author-life coach-speaker
Bell, Joshua, Violinist
Benz, Julie, Actress
Bertinelli, Valerie, Actress
Bisset, Jacqueline, Actress
Blyth, Catherine, Author
Boothman, Nicholas, Author-inspirational speaker
Brand, Russell, Comedian
Buck, Pearl S., Writer-novelist-Nobel Prize winner
Buscaglia, Leo F., Author-motivational speaker
Chanel, Coco, Fashion designer
Churchill, Winston, British statesman-Prime Minister-Nobel Prize winner
Clark, Frank A., Lawyer-politician
Cooper, Alan, Software designer-programmer
Coppola, Francis Ford, Film director-producer-screen writer
Couric, Katie, Broadcast journalist
Covey Stephen, Author-educator
Dalai Lama, Spiritual Leader of Tibetan Buddhism
Dasher, James, Writer
de la Fressange, Ines, Model-author-designer
de la Renta, Oscar, Fashion designer
Demarais, Ann, Author-first impression consultant

Di Giusto, Sylvie, Author-image consultant
Disney, Walt, Entrepreneur-animator-film producer
Dowe, Tracey, Success Coach
Duncan, Tim, Basketball player
Einstein, Albert, Theoretical physicist
Emerson, Ralph Waldo, Poet-essayist
Evert, Chris, Professional tennis player
Fergie, Singer-songwriter
Ford, Henry, Industrialist
Forni, Dr. P.M., Professor-author
Fosdick, Harry Emerson, Pastor
Franklin, Benjamin, American inventor-politician-statesman-diplomat
Fulk, Ken, Decorator-event designer
Gaga, Lady Singer-songwriter
Garland, Judy, Singer-actress
Gates, Bill, Microsoft co-founder-investor-author-philanthropist
Gates, Melinda, Businesswoman-philanthropist
Gibran, Khalil, Artist-poet-writer
Gish, Lillian, Actress
Guber, Peter, Film producer-educator-author
Guthrie, Catherine, Journalist-health writer
Hamilton Eleanor, Author-columnist-family therapist
Hanks, Tom, Actor
Haviland, Page, Ph.D., Psychologist
Hawn, Goldie, Actress
Heinlein, Robert A., Science fiction writer
Hemingway, Ernest, Novelist-journalist
Hepburn, Audrey, Actress
Heatherton, Erin, Fashion model-actress
Herrera, Carolina, Fashion designer
Hewlett, Sylvia Ann, Author-economist-consultant
Jacobi, Jeffrey, Public speaking coach
Jacobs, Marc, Fashion designer
Jewel, Singer-songwriter
Jobs, Steve, Apple co-founder-inventor-industrial designer

Kalantri, Amit, Actor
Karan, Donna, Fashion designer
Kawasaki, Guy, Author-speaker
Kay, Katy, Journalist
Keats, John, Poet
Keller, Helen, Author-activist-lecturer
Kennedy, John F., 35th U.S. President
King Jr., Dr. Martin Luther, Minister-activist
Klum, Heidi, Model
Koval, Robin, Writer-advertising executive
Kravitz, Zoe, Actress
Lauren, Ralph, Fashion designer-style icon
Lawrence, D.H., Writer
Lavington, Camille, Author-image consultant
Lennon, John, Singer-songwriter
Levine, Michael, Author
Lincoln, Abraham, 16th U.S. President
Lombardi, Vince, Football player-coach
Lovato, Demi, Singer-songwriter
Maharishi Mahesh, Yogi
Mandino, Og, Author-speaker
Manson, Marilyn, Singer-songwriter
Martin, Judith, Journalist-author-etiquette expert
Marston, Ralph, Writer-publisher
McCarthy, Melissa, Actress
McGonigal, Jane, Author-game designer
Meyer, Joyce, Author-speaker
Midler, Bette, Singer-songwriter-actress
Mizner, Wilson, Playwright
Morgan, Barbara, Teacher-astronaut
Mother Teresa, Nun-missionary-saint
Mridha, Debasish, Physician-poet-seer-author
Neimark, Ira, Author-retail executive
Ocean, Frank, Singer
Ohno, Apolo, Speed skater

Pavarotti, Luciano, opera singer
Peale, Norman Vincent, Author-minister
Perry, Katy, Singer-songwriter
Picasso, Pablo, Artist
Poe, Edgar Allen, Writer-poet
Portman, Natalie, Actress
Posey, A.D., Author
Post, Emily, Author-etiquette expert
Proske, Jenn, Actress
Ray, Rachel, Television personality-cook-author
Reagan, Nancy, U.S. First
Retton, Mary Lou, Gymnast
Rhames, Ving, Actor
Roosevelt, Franklin Delano, 32nd U.S. President
Salmansohn, Karen, Author
Sarandon, Susan, Actress
Sarnoff, Dorothy, Musical artist-image consultant
Schumer, Amy, Comedian-writer-actress-producer
Schweitzer, Albert, Theologian-philosopher-Nobel Peace Prize winner
Shakespeare, William, Poet-playwright
Sharapova, Maria, Professional tennis player
Shea, Robert, Author
Shipman, Claire, Journalist
Simpson-Giles, Candace, Author
Singer, Issac Bashevis, Writer, Nobel Prize winner
Smith, Will, Actor-comedian
Spade, Kate, Fashion designer
Stevenson, Robert Louis, Novelist-poet-essayist
Stoddard, Alexandra, Author-interior designer-lifestyle philosopher
Stone, Sharon, Actress
Swift, Taylor, Singer-songwriter
Talley, Andre Leon, Fashion editor
Tannen, Deborah, Academic-professor-author
Thaler, Linda Kaplan, Author-advertising executive
Thomas, Clarence, Supreme Court Justice

Tracy, Brian, Motivational speaker-self-development author
Twombly, Cy, Artist
Tzu, Lao, Philosopher
Vaswani, Dada, Philosopher
Vitale, Joe, Author-motivational speaker
Voltaire, Writer-historian-philosopher
Vongerichten, Jean-Georges, Restaurateur-chef-cookbook writer
Walters, Barbara, Broadcast journalist-author
Ward, William, Writer of inspirational maxims
Welch, Jack, Executive-author-chemical engineer
Welch, Suzy, Author-business journalist-public speaker
West, Kay, Actress
White, Valerie, Author-first impression consultant
Wilde, Oscar, Playwright-author
Wilson, Joni, Author-voice coach
Winfrey, Oprah, Multi-media icon
Wirthlin, Joseph B., Businessman-religious leader
Wood, Doris, Author-speaker-trainer-consultant
Wordsworth, William, Poet
Young, Loretta, Actress
Yousafzai, Malala, Education activist-Nobel Peace Prize winner
Zeta-Jones, Catherine, Actress
Ziglar, Zig, Author-motivational speaker
Zoe, Rachel, Fashion designer

Made in United States
North Haven, CT
22 October 2022

25776176R00072